I LIKE ART:

BAROQUE

Margaux Stanitsas

Published in the United States by Xist Publishing
www.xistpublishing.com
PO Box 61593 Irvine, CA 92602

© 2018 Text by Margaux Stanitsas
Images Licensed from Adobe Stock
and public domain artworks provided by
The Metropolitan Museum of Art, New York

First Edition
ISBN: 978-1-5324-0517-4
eISBN: 978-1-5324-0518-1

Table of Contents:

Baroque

I like art. I love painting and drawing.

It is fun to make my own art but it is also really interesting to learn about art from the past.

The different times people made art are sometimes called "periods."

The **Baroque** art period began around the year 1600.

Notice the dramatic, detailed figures. Do you see the bright highlights and dark shadows? Can you guess who this painting is of? It is Saint Peter. This is a Baroque painting.

Baroque art is known to be very elaborate and dramatic. The subjects of this art are often religious figures, mythological characters or wealthy patrons. Even the word "baroque" means detailed and ornate.

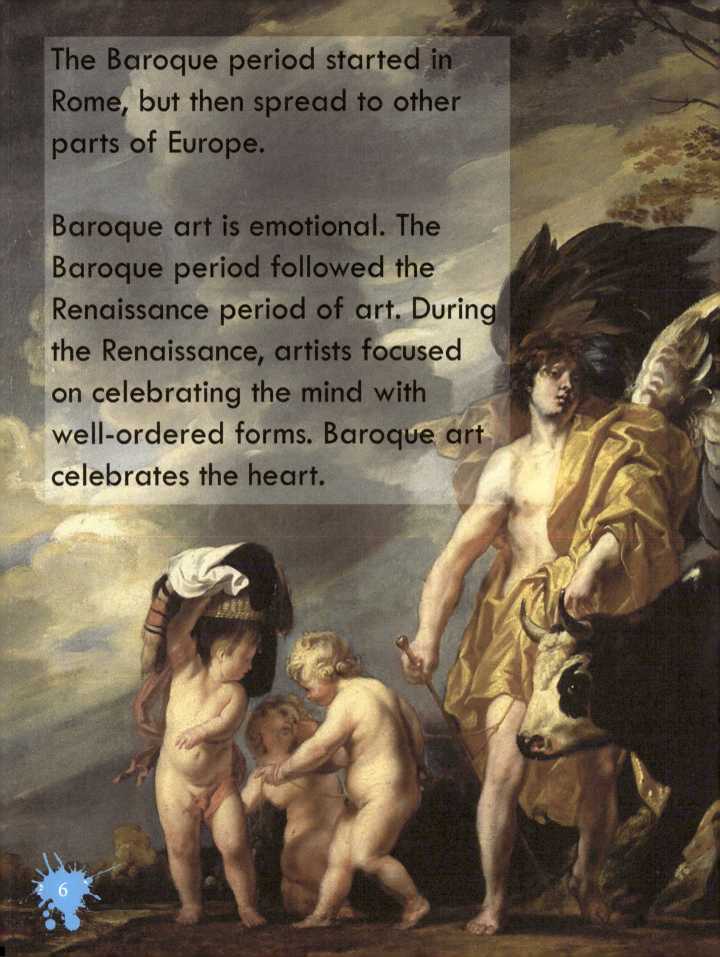

The Baroque period started in Rome, but then spread to other parts of Europe.

Baroque art is emotional. The Baroque period followed the Renaissance period of art. During the Renaissance, artists focused on celebrating the mind with well-ordered forms. Baroque art celebrates the heart.

The Influences

Baroque art was a response to the Reformation. The Reformation was a major event that affected Baroque art. The Reformation occurred when a man named Martin Luther decided to separate from the Catholic Church and create his own church. He wanted to reform, or change, the ways of the church.

Many people were leaving the Catholic Church at this time. Catholic leaders paid artists to paint beautiful pictures of religious things, so that they would make the Catholic Church look more appealing.

Baroque paintings from Catholic European countries are almost always religious. When religious figures are depicted, this style shows them as ordinary people in their regular daily activities.

Baroque paintings from Protestant Europe still have the same emotion and drama, but they are more likely to be still lifes and landscapes.

The Techniques

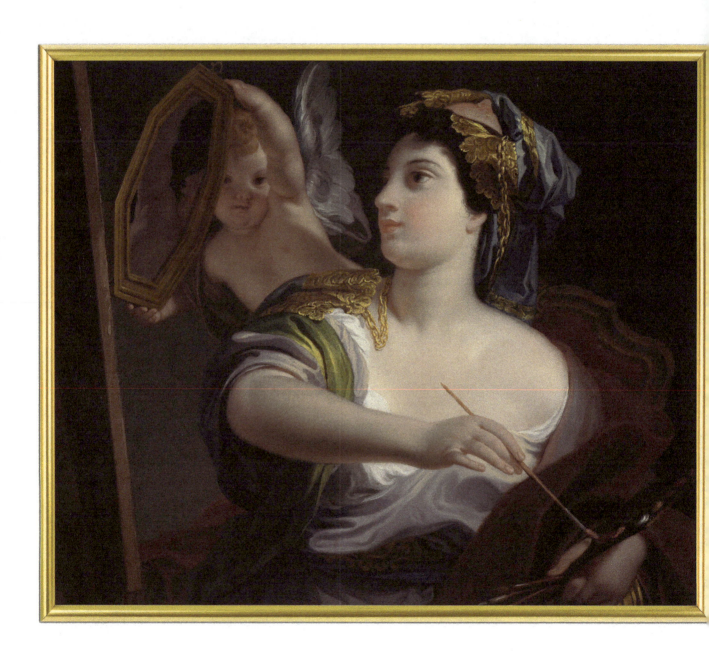

Baroque art is special in many ways. This type of art shows a lot of motion using diagonal lines and remarkable detail.

This style is meant to produce drama and show extravagance. Baroque art is meant to be emotional and enjoyed by all of the senses.

A very common technique used in Baroque style is the chiaroscuro [chi-ARO-scuu-row] technique. This is a way of painting light colors and dark colors to show the difference between them.

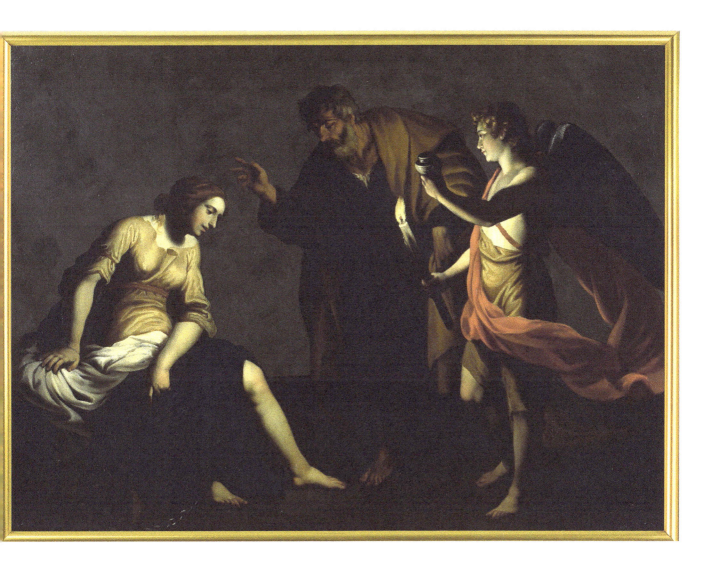

As you can see in this painting, most of it is dark, but the light parts are very bright. This adds drama and makes the important parts of the picture stand out.

Famous Artists

Peter Paul Rubens is a very important Baroque painter. His paintings feature lots of movement, color, and drama. His art has many characteristics that reveal that he was part of the counter-Reformation, which fought to keep the Catholic Church from changing. He usually painted religious or mythological figures, hunting scenes, or portraits of people he knew.

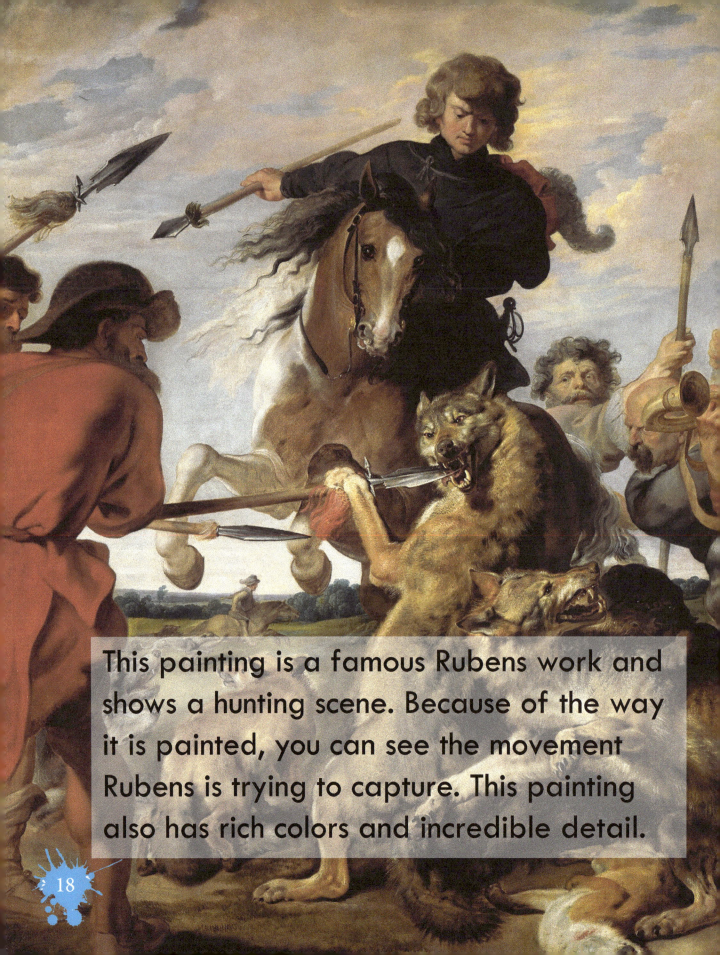

This painting is a famous Rubens work and shows a hunting scene. Because of the way it is painted, you can see the movement Rubens is trying to capture. This painting also has rich colors and incredible detail.

François De Nomé [Fran-swah deh-NO-may] is a French Baroque painter, who lived in Italy during this time. He usually includes dark skies and naturally toned colors in his paintings.

He also paints people very small. He has a very unique style of painting, which has inspired many other styles and artists after him.

20

This is a painting by De Nomé. It includes all his usual techniques. It has the tiny people, the dark sky, and the earth-tone colors. This is also an example of the dramatic Baroque style, showing over-the-top and extravagant architecture.

Francesco Guardi is another Baroque painter who used similar techniques to De Nomé. He painted large buildings and small people. But do you see the differences in his style? In this image, Guardi has painted the back of the building, instead of the front.

The Impact

Baroque style architecture and paintings are still kept in many cities all over the world, like Rome and Venice, Italy. The dramatic Baroque style is used to this day to decorate homes and buildings.

Your Turn

Now it's your turn to make a Baroque painting.

Will you paint something religious?
How will you communicate the focus of the painting?
Will you make the highlights bright?
The shadows dark?
How will you add drama and extravagance?

The Art

Virgin and Child with Saint Catherine of Alexandria
Anthony van Dyck
1630
Metropolitan Museum of Art, New York

The Abduction of Orithyia
Style of Francesco Solimena
1730
The Walters Art Museum, Baltimore

The Denial Of Saint Peter
Caravaggio
1610
Metropolitan Museum of Art, New York

Flight of the Holy Family into Egypt
Jacob Jordaens
1647
The Walters Art Museum, Baltimore

Portrait of Pope Clement XIII
Anton Raphael Mengs
1759
The Walters Art Museum, Baltimore

The Holy Family with Saint Elizabeth, Saint John, and a Dove
Peter Paul Rubens
1608
Metropolitan Museum of Art, New York

Wolf and Fox Hunt
Peter Paul Rubens
1616
Metropolitan Museum of Art, New York

Allegory of Painting
Domenico Corvi
1764
The Walters Art Museum, Baltimore

Saint Agatha Attended by Saint Peter and an Angel in Prison
Alessandro Turchi
1640
The Walters Art Museum, Baltimore

Christ and the Tribute Money
Domenico Fetti
1610
The Walters Art Museum, Baltimore

Flowers by a Pond with Frogs
Guiseppe Recco
1670-1679
The Walters Art Museum, Baltimore

A Venetian Courtyard
Francesco Guardi
1770's
The Walters Art Museum, Baltimore

St. Paul Preaching to the Corinthians
François de Nomé
1620
The Walters Art Museum, Baltimore

Mirror
German, Danzig (Gdansk)
1680-1700
Metropolitan Museum of Art, New York

Adoration of the Shepherds
Bernardo Strozzi
1615
The Walters Art Museum, Baltimore

Head of Saint John the Baptist Presented to Salome
François de Nomé
1620
The Walters Art Museum, Baltimore

Glossary

Chiaroscuro: A painting technique

Dramatic: emotional

Elaborate: something with many details

Extravagant: something that is very fancy

Landscape: A painting of nature

Ornate: complicated decoration

Patron: Someone who pays for art

Still Life: A painting of an arranged group of objects

Index